p p q r s t u v w x y z

First American Edition
Copyright © 1984 by John Burningham
All rights reserved
Published in 1984 by The Viking Press
40 West 23rd Street, New York, New York 10010
Published in Great Britain by Walker Books Ltd.
Printed in Italy
1 2 3 4 5 88 87 86 85 84
ISBN 0-670-65349-7
Library of Congress catalog card number: 83-23551
(CIP data available)

E
BUR

10|87

sniff shout

John Burningham

THE VIKING PRESS
NEW YORK

suck

shout

sob

cough

Snore

sniff

sneeze

whisper

whistle

scratch

lick

flap

yawn

gargle

abcdefghijklm